Savvy

Crafty Creations

Crochet Projects That Will Hook You

by Karen Whooley

CAPSTONE PRESS
a capstone imprint

Savvy Books are published by Capstone Press,
1710 Roe Crest Drive, North Mankato, Minnesota 56003
www.mycapstone.com

Library of Congress Cataloging-in-Publication Data
Names: Whooley, Karen, author.
Title: Crochet projects that will hook you / by Karen Whooley.
Description: North Mankato, Minnesota: Capstone Press, 2018. | Series:
    Crafty creations | Audience: Ages 9-13.
Identifiers: LCCN 2017043022 (print) | LCCN 2017044401 (eBook) | ISBN
    9781515774518 (eBook PDF) | ISBN 9781515774471 (hardcover)
Subjects: LCSH: Crocheting–Patterns–Juvenile literature.
Classification: LCC TT825 (eBook) | LCC TT825 .W5523 2018 (print) | DDC
    746.43/4–dc23
LC record available at https://lccn.loc.gov/2017043022

Editorial Credits
Mari Bolte, editor; Juliette Peters, designer; Sarah Schuette, photo stylist;
Marcy Morin, scheduler; Kathy McColley, production specialist;
Karen Whooley and Marcie Spence, project creators

Photo Credits
Capstone Studio: Karon Dubke, 2-3, 4, 6, 7, 10, 11, 12, 13, 14, 15, 16-17, 18 (top),
20, 23 (bottom), 24 (top), 26 (right), 27, 28 (top), 31 (middle and bottom), 32,
33 (middle right and bottom left), 35, 36, 37 (middle right and bottom left),
39 (bottom), 42 (right), 43, 44, 45, 48, TJ Thoraldson Digital Photography, 18
(bottom), 19, 21, 22, 23 (top and middle), 24 (bottom), 25, 26 (left and middle), 28
(bottom), 29, 30, 31 (top), 33 (top and bottom right), 34, 37 (top and bottom right),
38, 39 (top), 40, 41, 42 (left); Juliette Peters, 8, 9; Shutterstock: Claudia Paulussen,
cover (top), gabriel12, cover (bottom)

Printed and bound in the USA.
010845S18

Table of Contents

Get Started!

Get lost in yards of yarn! Crochet your way to blankets, bags, and bunting as you learn to read traditional patterns. Once you've mastered the basic moves, take on patterns for the advanced beginner and beyond. Each stitch is another step in becoming a crochet expert!

Tools

You'll need a few simple tools to get started. Look for crochet supplies in craft or yarn stores, or online.

Crochet Hooks

You can't crochet without a hook! Crochet hooks are made from a variety of materials, including aluminum, plastic, wood, bamboo, and steel. The United States uses a letter and number system for determining hook sizes. Other countries use a metric system that labels the actual circumference of the hook.

The projects in this book were all made with a size H/8 (5.0mm) hook.

Measuring Tape

Having a measuring tape is a must in order to take accurate measurements. It will help you check your stitch and row gauge.

Yarn Needle

A good, blunt metal yarn needle is important to weave in ends. Plastic needles don't work as well; they tend to be too large and can damage the yarn. When you purchase yours make sure that the eye of the needle is big enough to thread the yarn through.

Row Counter

These handy tools are great to help keep track of the number of rows you have made. If a pattern calls for two of something this is a good way to know how many rows you made the first time.

Yarn

Yarns range from fine strands to bulky textures. The projects in this book were created using easy-to-find *Super Saver* yarn, made by *Red Heart*. It is a good yarn to use when learning how to crochet. Although we listed the yarn colors we used, feel free to change the colors to your favorites.

For similar results, find a yarn labeled "4" on the Yarn Standard Weight System chart.

Yarn labels also tell you the recommended hook size(s) for that yarn, based on the Yarn Standard Weight System. But keep in mind that they are just recommendations. You will still have to find the hook size that works for you to get the finished project to be the size you need.

An organization called the *Craft Yarn Council* created a standard system to organize yarns by weight and thickness. This is called the Yarn Standard Weight System.

Yarn Weight	Recommended Hook U.S. Sizes
0 LACE	Steel: 6, 7, 8 or Regular: B-1
1 SUPER FINE	B-1 to E-4
2 FINE	E-4 to 7
3 LIGHT	7 to I-9
4 MEDIUM	I-9 to K-10 1/2
5 BULKY	K-10 1/2 to M-13
6 SUPER BULKY	M-13 to Q
7 JUMBO	Q and larger

Yarn can be made from all kinds of fiber. Some yarn comes from animals, some from plants, and some are synthetic.

The most popular fiber for crochet is wool that comes from sheep, but there is also wool that is made from alpaca, llama, musk ox, rabbit (angora), goat (cashmere), camel, possum, and silkworms (silk). Some people even spin wool from their dog's fur! Plant-based yarns include cotton, linen (from flax), hemp, soy, and bamboo.

Acrylic (synthetic) yarns are affordable and available in different colors and textures. These won't be as warm as a wool, but they are a great choice for beginners. Choose yarns that are smooth and simple when you are starting out. Save fuzzy or frilly yarn for later.

skein

hank

Most yarn comes in a ready-to-use ball, called a skein. Surprisingly, these short, oval-shaped skeins don't really look like balls at all!

If your yarn comes in a hank, ask the shop where you bought it if they can wind it into a cake for you. Cakes sit flat and won't get tangled as you crochet.

To wind your own cake, find a partner who can hold the big loop of yarn on their hands while you wind it into a ball. You can also use the back of a chair, or your knees.

Gauge

Gauge – the number of stitches and rows in each inch – is the single most important part of producing a crochet project of a specific size. But there are many factors, from yarn and hook size to weather and emotions, which can change your personal crochet tension. A change in crochet tension can change your project's gauge.

To accurately measure gauge in these patterns, start by crocheting about 4 inches (10.2 centimeters) of the project. Then place your measuring tape along the edge. Compare it to the number of stitches that you need based on the gauge given you in the pattern. If you have too few stitches, get a smaller hook. If you have too many, grab a bigger hook. But if you are within a millimeter or two of the projected size, then you can keep the original hook.

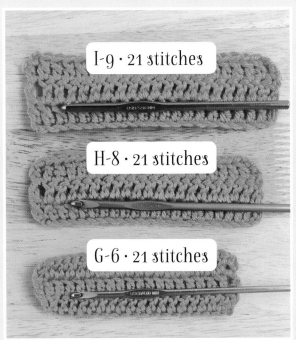

I-9 · 21 stitches

H-8 · 21 stitches

G-6 · 21 stitches

Crochet Hook Sizes

U.S. Size	Millimeter Range
B-1	2.25mm
C-2	2.75 mm
D-3	3.25 mm
E-4	3.5 mm
F-5	3.75 mm
G-6	4 mm
7	4.5mm
H-8	5 mm
I-9	5.5 mm
J-10	6 mm
K-101/2	6.5 mm
L-11	8 mm
M/N-13	9 mm
N/P-15	10 mm
P/Q	15 mm
Q	16 mm
S	19 mm

But before you change hooks, also measure the number of rows per inch in the piece. Use the same rules you used with the stitches to determine if your hook is the right size.

Sometimes gauge can be off in only one direction. This is a common issue! If the stitches per inch are off, change your hook. But if the rows are off, keep the hook. If you had too many stitches, crochet more loosely. If you had too few, crochet more tightly.

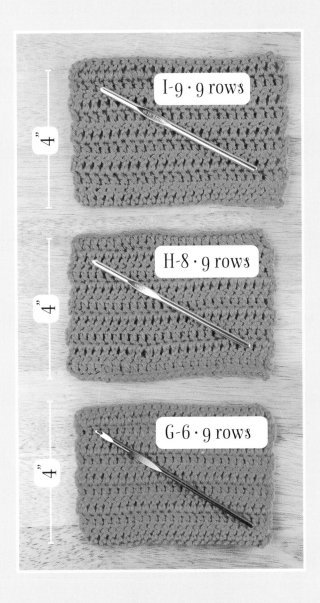

I-9 · 9 rows

4"

H-8 · 9 rows

4"

G-6 · 9 rows

4"

How to Hold the Hook

There are two main methods of holding a crochet hook – pencil hold or knife hold. Try them both to see which one feels most comfortable to you. Everyone is different in how they hold their hooks.

The Pencil Hold

Place the hook in your right hand, holding it between your index finger and thumb, as you would a pencil.

The Knife Hold

Hold the hook in your right hand with an overhand hold, similar to the way you might hold a knife.

How to Make a Slip Knot

The slip knot is the first thing you do before you start any project. Most patterns don't even include this in the instructions because it is assumed that you already know this. The starting slip knot is never counted as a stitch. The first couple of patterns will remind you, but later projects will leave it out, like normal patterns found elsewhere.

Tip:
You can pull the slipknot's tail to adjust the size of the loop to slide over the crochet hook.

1. To make a slip knot to fit the hook, shape the yarn like a pretzel.

2. Slip the hook into the pretzel.

3. Pull down on both ends of the yarn to tighten the knot.

How to Hold the Yarn

Hold the hook in your right hand while keeping an even tension on the yarn with your left hand. To control the tension of your yarn, drape it over your index finger. This will help you easily adjust how tightly or loosely you crochet.

How to Fasten Off

When you reach the end of a project, you'll need to know how to fasten off. Cut the yarn at least 6 inches (15.2 cm) from the end of the project. Draw the yarn through the last loop. Gently pull on the tail to tighten. This will prevent unraveling.

Weaving in Ends

Before your crochet project is complete, you must finish off all your yarn ends. This means weaving in all the yarn ends securely so they don't unravel. If using a pattern and solid color yarn, you can work over yarn ends as you go.

You can weave in your ends anywhere. But there are a few important things to remember while weaving in your ends:
· make sure they are encased within the stitches
· make sure they don't show
· be sure to weave them in at least three times

Thread the yarn end through a yarn needle. Position the yarn at the base of a row of stitches. Then weave 1 inch in one direction, 1 inch in the reverse direction, and then back the original direction again. Cut off excess yarn.

Tip:
Weave in only one yarn end at a time to avoid a bulky spot in your work.

These are the basics! Now let's move on to the patterns and learning to crochet!

Let's Crochet!

Pick a project and get going! Start simple and then challenge yourself to create something you've never tried before. Give your finished pieces away, or keep them to show off your work.

Stitched Shoelaces

Abbreviations You Should Know:

ch – Chain: When reading a crochet pattern, you will see instructions such as Ch 20. That means you should make 20 chains. Remember that the loop that is on your hook does not count as one of the chains.

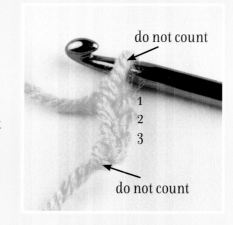

do not count

1
2
3

do not count

These shoelaces will not only decorate your shoes, they will teach you the first stitch in order to crochet – the chain stitch. Many crochet projects start with a chain. You'll find this basic stitch everywhere!

Materials

small amount of *Red Heart Yarns Super Saver* in the color Glowworm

US Size H/8 (5mm) crochet hook

one shoelace to use to measure the length

What else can you use these shoelaces for?

• Make them shorter to tie in your hair.

• Make them longer to make a bow on a present.

1 Make a slip knot.

2 Put your hook in the slip knot loop and pull the tail until the loop is small enough to stay on the hook, but with a little bit of space to pull the hook and yarn through.

3 Start making a chain. Holding the base of the slip knot with your thumb and middle finger of your left hand, wrap yarn from back of the hook over and around the front of the hook. Then pull yarn through the loop to form the first chain. This wrap and pull is called a "Yarn Over".

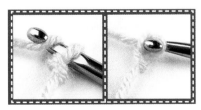

4 Repeat step 3 to make additional chain stitches. Keep going until your chain is the same length as your shoelace. (Do not include the tail that you have at the beginning of the chain.)

5 Fasten off.

6 Count the number of chains in the crocheted shoelace so you can make a second one the same length.

7 You can cut the tails at the ends a little shorter so that they aren't in the way when you wear your shoes. Just don't cut them too short – no less than ¾-inch-long. Too short and the laces will unravel.

Mitts For Me

Abbreviations You Should Know:

sc - Single Crochet. The abbreviation "sc" in a pattern means you should make a single crochet. "2 sc" means to make two single crochets. You might even see a larger number.

These mitts are worked flat, and then sewn up for a custom fit. Learn the single crochet stitch – the second stitch all crocheters learn. Make a pair of mitts for anyone in your family!

Materials

60-100 yards of *Red Heart Yarns Super Saver* in the color Cherry Red

US Size H/8 (5mm) crochet hook

yarn needle

Tip:
Have a notecard or sticky note handy to jot down measurements and chain lengths.

Tip:
Remember that the slip knot does not count as a chain!

1 Take two measurements of your hands:

a the length from the first knuckle of the pointer finger to 2.5 inches below the wrist

b the circumference of the hand

2 Make a chain that matches the first measurement.

3 Count the number of chains you just made. Write the number down – you'll need it later! Add one extra chain at the end. This is called a turning chain. It is used to keep the sides straight and to make sure you start your row at the right height.

4 For the first row, we are going to skip the last chain we made. In the second chain, you are going to do the following:

a: Insert your hook into the chain.

• One of the most common ways to begin to crochet stitches is to have the front of the foundation row facing you (the Vs).

• Insert the hook into the center of the Vs and under the back bar.

b: Yarn over and pull the loop through the chain. Now you have 2 loops on your hook.

Continued on the next page...

21

c: Yarn over and pull through both the loops on your hook. Your first single crochet is now complete.

5 Continue by making one single crochet in each chain across to the end. Once you get to the end, row one is done. You should have the same number of stitches as you did in step 3.

6 For row 2 and all the remaining rows you will do the following:

a: Chain 1. Turn your work so that you can work back across the top of the stitches you just made.

b: If you look at the top of the stitches, you will see another chain. Each "chain" is one stitch.

c: You are going to ignore that chain you just made.

d: In the first stitch you will repeat steps 4a–4c. The only difference is that you will work in the hole right underneath the chain on the top of each stitch. At the end of each row you should have the same number of stitches as the number you wrote down in step 3.

7 Keep making rows until the length of the fabric is the same length as the circumference of your hand. You will measure from the bottom of row one to the top of the last row you made.

8 When the mitt is complete, fasten off. Leave a tail of 18 inches when you cut the yarn. This will be used to sew up the mitt.

9 To sew up the mitt, put the 18-inch tail on a needle. Whipstitch the sides of the top and bottom edge together. Match the stitches on each side until you reach where you want the bottom of the thumb to be. Weave in the tail a bit to end it off (and cut). Skip three stitches on each side and whipstitch to the top.

10 Weave in all the ends and turn the mitt right-side-out. You are done with the first mitt.

11 Now repeat everything for the second mitt.

How to Whipstitch

1 Position the pieces with right sides facing each other.

2 Match the first two stitches of the pieces together. Insert the needle and pull the yarn through the inside loops.

3 Draw the needle up and over the 2 loops of the first stitch. Don't pull too hard or you will gather the fabric.

4 Repeat steps 2 and 3 until all the edges are joined.

5 At the end of the seam, weave the yarn back through several stitches to secure.

6 Turn the project right-side-out.

Pom-Pom Hat

Finished Size:

circumference and 12 inches tall before pom-pom and folding the brim.

This hat pattern will fit heads from 16 inches to 21 inches in circumference.

Gauge:

measuring the half double crochet portion

3 stitches = 1 inch

2 ½ rows = 1 inch

Abbreviations You Should Know:

rs - Right Side. When the project is done, you will show this side of the work.

hdc - Half Double Crochet. When reading a crochet pattern, you will see the abbreviation "hdc". This means you should do a half double crochet. "2 hdc" means to make 2 half double crochets.

BLO - Back Loop Only. This is used while working across the top of the stitches in the chain that is made on top of each stitch. Insert your hook in the part of the chain that is farthest away from you. This creates a ridge on the fabric that adds texture.

back loop

front loop

Some yarns are dyed multiple colors. They are known as variegated yarns. Start using them to make a pom-pom hat! This project will also introduce you to reading real crochet patterns.

Materials

120 yards of *Red Heart Yarns Super Saver* in the color Day Glow

US Size H/8 (5mm) crochet hook

yarn needle

additional yarn (for the pom-pom)

1 Chain 42.

2 For the first row, you are going to skip the last two chains you made. In the third chain, you are going to do the following to create your first half double crochet:

    a: Yarn over and then insert your hook into the chain.

    b: Yarn over and pull the loop through the chain. Now you have 3 loops on your hook.

    c: Yarn over and pull through all three loops on your hook. Your first half double crochet is now complete.

    d: This row is the right side.

3 Continue by making half double crochets in the next 31 chains. There should be 8 chains left.

4 Make a single crochet in each of the last 8 chains. You should have 32 half double crochets and 8 single crochets.

This will complete the row. The single crochets you made will help taper the hat at the top.

Continued on the next page...

5 For row 2:

a: Chain 1 and turn.

b: If you look at the top of the stitches, you will see another chain. Each "chain" is one stitch.

c: Ignore that chain you just made.

d: Working in the back loop only, single crochet in the first 8 single crochets.

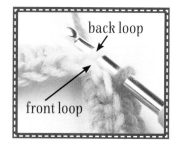

e: Working in the back loop only, half double crochet in the remaining 32 stitches.

6 For row 3:

a: Chain 2 and turn.

b: Ignore that chain 2 you just made.

c: Working in the back loop only, half double crochet in the first 32 stitches then single crochet in the last 8 stitches.

7 For row 4, just repeat row 2.

8 For rows 5-34, repeat rows 3 and 4 fifteen times.

9 When the hat is complete, fasten off. Leave a 24-inch tail when you cut the yarn. This is needed to sew up the hat.

10 With right sides facing, whipstitch the two edges together. Use the remaining tail to weave in and out of the edge of the single crochet rows and pull tight to gather the top.

11 Use the tails to attach the pom-pom. Weave in all ends. Flip up the brim and you are done!

To make a pom-pom:

1 Gently wrap yarn around your hand.

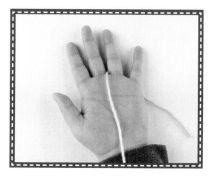

2 Wrap the yarn between 90 and 100 times. Cut off the end.

3 Loop a piece of yarn around the wraps and tie it tightly to make a bow shape. Cut off the excess.

Tip:

"Turn" means you should turn your work. This will allow you to work back across the top of the stitches you just made.

4 Slip the yarn off your hand and cut the looped ends with scissors.

5 Use the scissors to trim the yarn into a round pom-pom shape.

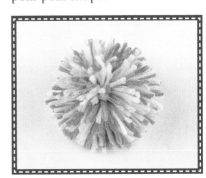

Now for the "real" pattern!

This is what patterns you buy will look like. Compare the numbered steps and the photos to the pattern below.

Pom-Pom Hat

Ch 42.

Row 1: (rs) Hdc in 3rd ch from hook and in next 31 ch, sc in last 8 ch.

Row 2: Ch 1, turn, working in the BLO, sc in each sc, hdc in each hdc.

Row 3: Ch 2, turn, working in the BLO, hdc in each hdc, sc in each sc.

Row 4: Repeat row 2.

Rows 5–34: Repeat rows 3 and 4 fifteen times more. At the end of row 34, fasten off leaving a 24-inch tail for sewing.

Skipped Scarf

Finished Size:
54 inches long by
7 inches wide

Gauge:
2 ¾ stitches = 1 inch
row gauge is
not important
in this pattern

Abbreviations You Should Know:

dc - Double Crochet. When reading a crochet pattern, you will see the abbreviation "dc". This means you should make a double crochet. You might even see "2 dc" which means to make two double crochets. It could be even a larger number.

sk - Skip. It means to skip the stitch the pattern calls you to skip.

skip
correct

This scarf is fun to make because you can control the length. The instructions use less than a full skein of yarn. Use it all to make a longer scarf.

Materials

236 yards of *Red Heart Yarns Super Saver* in the color Banana Berry

US Size H/8 (5mm) crochet hook

yarn needle

Tip:

Have a notecard or sticky note handy to jot down measurements and chain lengths.

1 Chain 21.

2 For the first row, skip the last two chains we made. In the third chain, you are going to do the following to create your first double crochet:

a: Yarn over and then insert your hook into the chain.

b: Yarn over and pull the loop through the chain. Now you have 3 loops on your hook.

c: Yarn over and pull through the first 2 loops on your hook. Now you have 2 loops left on your hook.

d: Yarn over and pull through both loops left on the hook. This will complete your double crochet.

3 Continue by making double crochets all the way across. When you are done with the row, there should be 19 double crochets.

Continued on the next page...

29

4 For row 2:

a: Chain 2 and turn.

b: Double crochet in the first 2 double crochets. Note that you are skipping over the chain 2 you just made. This will happen now on every row.

c: Chain one.

d: Skip over the next double crochet. (This will make a space.)

e: Double crochet in the next double crochet.

f: Repeat steps c through e six more times.

g: Repeat steps c and d.

h: Double crochet in the last 2 double crochets. Row 2 is now complete.

5 For row 3:

a: Chain 2 and turn.

b: Double crochet in the first 2 double crochets.

c: Chain one.

d: Skip over the next chain. (This makes a space on top of the previous space.)

e: Double crochet in the next double crochet.

f: Repeat steps c through e six more times.

g: Repeat steps c and d.

h: Double crochet in the last 2 double crochets. Row 3 is now complete.

6 Repeat row 3 until your scarf is as long as you want it to be, not including the last 2 rows of the scarf.

7 Next row:

a: Chain 2 and turn.

b: Double crochet in the first 2 double crochets.

c: Double crochet in the next space.

d: Double crochet in the next double crochet.

e: Repeat steps c and d six times.

f: Double crochet in the next space and in the last 2 dc.

8 Last row:

a: Chain 2 and turn.

b: Double crochet in each stitch across.

Fasten off.

Weave in all the ends to finish the scarf.

Skipped Scarf

Ch 21

Row 1: Dc in 3rd ch from hook and in each ch across.

Row 2: Ch 2 (ch 2 does not count as a stitch now and throughout), turn; dc in first 2 dc, ch 1, (sk next dc, dc in next dc, ch 1) 7 times, sk next dc and dc in last 2 dc.

Row 3: Ch 2, turn, dc in first 2 dc, ch 1, (sk next chain, dc in next dc, ch 1) 7 times, sk next dc and dc in last 2 dc.

Repeat row 3 until scarf is just 2 rows short of desired length.

Next row: Ch 2, turn, dc in each dc and chain space across.

Last row: Ch 2, turn, dc in each dc across. Fasten off.

Weave in all ends.

Color-Changing Cozy

Finished Size:

46 inches long by
41 inches wide

Gauge:

3 stitches = 1 inch
3 rows = 1 inch

Now that you have mastered the main stitches and know how to read a pattern, this blanket will be an easy project. You will learn to change colors and how to cross double crochet stitches to add texture.

Materials

1 skein each of *Red Heart Yarns Super Saver* in the colors (A) Royal, (B) Lavender, (C) WIldflower

US Size H/8 (5mm) crochet hook

yarn needle

With color A, ch 137.

Row 1: Sc in 2nd ch from hook and in each ch across. (136 sc)

Row 2: Ch 2, turn, sk first sc, dc in each st across.

NOTE: Ch 2 at the beginning of this row and every row following is counted as a double crochet. You will work into the top of the chain in the next row of single crochet so that you don't lose a stitch.

Row 3: Ch 1, turn, sc in each dc across. In last stitch, change to color B.

NOTE: Here is how to change colors:

1 Make the single crochet to the point of having the 2 loops on the hook with the old color.

2 Finish the single crochet with the new color.

Row 4: Ch 1, turn, sc in each sc across.

Row 5: Ch 2, turn, sk first sc, dc in each sc across.

Row 6: Ch 1, turn, sc in each dc across. In last stitch, change to color C.

Continued on the next page...

Row 7: Ch 1, turn, sc in each sc across.

Row 8: Ch 2, turn, sk first sc, dc in next sc, *sk next sc, dc in next sc,

dc in sc just skipped (this creates a "crossed stitch");

repeat from * across until 2 sc are left, dc in last 2 dc.

Row 9: Ch 1, turn, sc in each dc across. In last stitch, change to color B.

Row 10: Ch 1, turn, sc in each sc across.

Row 11: Ch 2, turn, sk first sc, dc in each st across.

Row 12: Ch 1, turn, sc in each dc across. In last stitch, change to color A.

Row 13: Ch 1, turn, sc in each sc across.

Row 14: Ch 2, turn, sk first sc, dc in each st across.

Row 15: Ch 1, turn, sc in each dc across. In last stitch, change to color C.

Row 16: Ch 1, turn, sc in each sc across.

Row 17: Ch 2, turn, sk first sc, dc in next sc, *sk next sc, dc in next sc, dc in sc just skipped (this creates a "crossed stitch"); repeat from * across until 2 sc are left, dc in last 2 dc.

Row 18: Ch 1, turn, sc in each dc across. In last stitch, change to color A.

Row 19: Ch 1, turn, sc in each sc across.

Row 20: Ch 2, turn, sk first sc, dc in each st across.

Row 21: Ch 1, sc in each dc across. In last stitch, change to color B.

Repeat rows 4-21 five times and then rows 4-15 once more. At end of last row, change to color C.

Edging:

Row 1: With color C, ch 1, turn, sc in each sc across to last sc, 3 sc in last sc, now working down the sides of the rows, evenly space 138 sc by working 2 sc in each dc row and 1 sc in each sc row, now working across bottom edge, 3 sc in first ch, sc in next 134 ch, 3 sc in last ch, working up the rows on the final side evenly space 138 sc working as done on previous side of rows, 2 sc in same sc as first sc.

Row 2: Do not turn work, sc in every sc around the blanket. Slip st in first sc of rnd. Fasten off.

Weave in all ends.

Pillow

Finished Size:
14 inches by
14 inches

Gauge:
3 ¼ stitches = 1 inch
3 rows = 1 inch

36

You might recognize the pattern – it's a smaller version of the blanket we made before. This time, you are going to learn to seam with a single crochet edging.

Materials

1 skein each of *Red Heart Yarns Super Saver* in the colors (A) Royal, (B) Lavender, (C) Wildflower

US Size H/8 (5mm) crochet hook

14-inch stuffed pillow form

yarn needle

Panel: (make 2)

With color A, ch 45.

Row 1: Sc in 2nd ch from hook and in each ch across. (44 sc)

Row 2 (rs): Ch 2, turn, sk first sc, dc in each sc across.

NOTE: Ch 2 at the beginning of this row and every row following is counted as a double crochet. You will work into the top of the chain in the next row of single crochet so that you don't lose a stitch.

Row 3: Ch 1, turn, sc in each dc across. In last stitch, change to color B.

NOTE: Here is how to change colors:

1 Make the single crochet to the point of having the 2 loops on the hook with the old color.

2 Finish the single crochet with the new color.

Row 4: Ch 1, turn, sc in each sc across.

Row 5: Ch 2, turn, sk first sc, dc in each sc across.

Row 6: Ch 1, turn, sc in each dc across. In last stitch, change to color C.

Row 7: Ch 1, turn, sc in each sc across.

Row 8: Ch 2, turn, sk first sc, dc in next sc, *sk next sc, dc in next sc,

dc in sc just skipped (this creates a "crossed stitch");

repeat from * across until 2 sc are left, dc in last 2 dc.

Row 9: Ch 1, turn, sc in each dc across. In last stitch, change to color B.

Row 10: Ch 1, turn, sc in each sc across.

Row 11: Ch 2, turn, sk first sc, dc in each sc across.

Row 12: Ch 1, turn, sc in each dc across. In last stitch, change to color A.

Row 13: Ch 1, turn, sc in each sc across.

Row 14: Ch 2, turn, sk first sc, dc in each sc across.

Row 15: Ch 1, turn, sc in each dc across. In last stitch, change to color C.

Row 16: Ch 1, turn, sc in each sc across.

Row 17: Ch 2, turn, sk first sc, dc in next sc, *sk next sc, dc in next sc, dc in sc just skipped (this creates a "crossed stitch"); repeat from * across until 2 sc are left; dc in last 2 dc.

Row 18: Ch 1, turn, sc in each dc across. In last stitch, change to color A.

Row 19: Ch 1, turn, sc in each sc across.

Row 20: Ch 2, turn, sk first sc, dc in each st across.

Row 21: Ch 1, turn, sc in each dc across. In last stitch, change to color B.

Rows 24-39: Repeat rows 10-21 once then 10-15 once more. At the end of row 39, change to color C.

Edging:

Row 1: Ch 1, turn, sc in each sc across to last sc, 3 sc in last sc, now working down the side of the rows, evenly space 42 sc by working 2 sc in each dc row and 1 sc in each sc row, now working across bottom edge, 3 sc in first ch, sc in next 42 ch, 3 sc in last ch, working up the rows on the final side evenly space 42 sc working as done on previous side of rows, 2 sc in same sc as first sc.

On first panel:

Fasten off and weave in the ends.

On second panel only:

Row 2: Weave in all the ends – except the working yarn – for the edging. Do not turn. Put wrong sides of the two panels together, starting with the corners you have matched up.

Then sc through both pieces of fabric around the first 3 sides. Insert the pillow form and then sc down the last side. Fasten off and weave in ends.

Bangles and Bunting

Finished Size:

46 inches long by
41 inches wide

Gauge:

3 stitches = 1 inch
3 rows = 1 inch

Abbreviations You Should Know:

sc2tog- Single crochet 2 together – Insert hook in next stitch, yarn over, and draw up a loop (2 loops on hook). Insert hook in next stitch, yarn over, and draw up a loop. Then yarn over and draw through all 3 loops on hook.

sc3tog- Single crochet 3 together – (Insert hook in next stitch, yarn over and draw up a loop) 3 times. Then yarn over and draw through all 4 loops on hook.

This fun-to-make hanging strip of triangles is fast and easy. Plus, you'll get to learn about how to decrease a bit. What colors would you choose?

Materials

1 skein each of *Red Heart Yarns Super Saver* in the colors Honeydew, Coral, Turqua and Aran

US Size H/8 (5mm) crochet hook

yarn needle

Triangles: (make 8, 2 in each color)

Ch 20.

Row 1: Sc in 2nd ch from hook and in each ch across. (19 sts)

Row 2: Ch 1, turn, sc in first sc, sc2tog, sc in each sc across to last 3 sc, sc2tog, sc in last stitch. (17 sts)

Row 3: Ch 1, turn, sc in each sc across.

Row 4: Ch 1, turn, sc in first sc, sc2tog, sc in each sc across to last 3 sc, sc2tog, sc in last stitch. (15 sts)

Row 5: Ch 1, turn, sc in each sc across.

Row 6: Ch 1, turn, sc in first sc, sc2tog, sc in each sc across to last 3 sc, sc2tog, sc in last stitch. (13 sts)

Row 7: Ch 1, turn, sc in each sc across.

Row 8: Ch 1, turn, sc in first sc, sc2tog, sc in each sc across to last 3 sc, sc2tog, sc in last stitch. (11 sts)

Row 9: Ch 1, turn, sc in each sc across.

Row 10: Ch 1, turn, sc in first sc, sc2tog, sc in each sc across to last 3 sc, sc2tog, sc in last stitch. (9 sts)

Row 11: Ch 1, turn, sc in each sc across.

Row 12: Ch 1, turn, sc in first sc, sc2tog, sc in each sc across to last 3 sc, sc2tog, sc in last stitch. (7 sts)

Row 13: Ch 1, turn, sc in each sc across.

Row 14: Ch 1, turn, sc in first sc, sc2tog, sc in each sc across to last 3 sc, sc2tog, sc in last stitch. (5 sts)

Row 15: Ch 1, turn, sc in each sc across.

Row 16: Ch 1, turn, sc in first sc, sc3tog, sc in last stitch. (3 sts)

Row 17: Ch 1, turn, sc in each sc across.

Row 18: Ch 1, turn, sc3tog. Fasten off.

Weave in all ends. Using any color you like, thread yarn onto yarn needle, keeping the end attached to the skein of yarn. String the two corners of the wide end of each triangle onto the yarn. Cut the yarn long enough so that you can use the tails to tack up the bunting at either end.

Try This

· Light it up! Poke holiday lights through the corners of each triangle. Use yarn bows to keep the lights secure. Decorate with stickers for a fun addition.

Try This

· Connect your triangles with crochet! Use a larger hook, such as a size L, and chain all your yarns. Attach the chain to the triangles by inserting your hook through a corner and including it in the chain. Chain three. In the next chain, attach it to the triangle. Chain three. Continue to the end of the triangle. Chain three, then repeat the process to attach the next triangle. Continue until all your triangles are attached.

To make the tassles, cut 8-inch lengths of each yarn. Fold the yarn in half, and then fold it between the triangles. Loop the ends of the yarn through the folds, and pull gently to tighten.

How to **sc2tog**

Single crochet 2 together

1 Insert hook in next stitch, yarn over, and draw up a loop (2 loops on hook).

2 Insert hook in next stitch, yarn over, and draw up a loop (3 loops on hook).

3 Then yarn over and draw through all 3 loops on hook.

sc3tog

Single crochet 3 together

1 Follow above instructions steps 1 through 2.

2 Repeat step 2 one more time. You will now have 4 loops on your hook.

3 Then yarn over and draw through all 4 loops on hook.

Bring-It-With Bag

Take your crochet projects anywhere with this crochet bag that you (surprise!) crochet yourself.

Materials

1 skein each of *Red Heart Yarns Super Saver* in the colors (A) Pink Camo and (B) Cafe Latte

US Size H/8 (5mm) crochet hook

yarn needle

Sides: (make 2)

With color A, ch 41.

Row 1: Dc in 3rd ch from hook and in each ch across. (40 dc)

NOTE: The skipped ch-2 counts as a dc.

Row 2 (rs): Ch 2, turn, dc in 2nd dc and in each dc across. (40 dc)

NOTE: Ch 2 at the beginning of each row counts as a dc.

Rows 3–24: Repeat row 2. Fasten off.

Handles: (make 2)

With Color B, ch 6.

Row 1: Sc in 2nd ch from hook and in each ch across. (5 sc)

Row 2: Ch 2, turn, sc in each sc across. (5 sc)

Repeat row 2 until handle is 22 inches in length. Fasten off.

Finishing:

Weave in all ends. Sew one handle onto each side on the right side of the fabric. Place the end of the strap about 5 inches down on either side, leaving a 12-inch loop.

Put the wrong sides together starting at one top corner on the long side of the bag, join with color B using a sc, then place 2 sc in the side of each row. Work through both pieces of fabric, matching rows as you go, all the way to the bottom. Then sc through both pieces of fabric along the bottom, all the way across to the other end matching chains as you go. Work up the other side of the bag by putting 2 sc in the sides of each row, working through both pieces of fabric (matching rows as you go). At the top, put one more sc in the corner, then fasten off.

Weave in ends.

Crochet Abbreviations Master List

Common abbreviations used in patterns can be hard to figure out at first. Keep this handy list available to look at while you crochet. Yarn industry designers and publishers may also use special abbreviations that you might not find here. You will see them called out at the beginning of the book or the pattern.

()	work instructions within parentheses as many times as directed	inc	increase
*	repeat the instructions following the asterisk as directed	lp(s)	loops
"	inch(es)	m	meter(s)
		MC	main color
alt	alternate	mm	millimeter(s)
beg	begin/beginning	oz	ounce(s)
BL	back loop(s)	pm	place marker
CA	color A	prev	previous
CB	color B	rem	remain/remaining
ch	chain stitch	rep	repeat(s)
ch-	refers to chain or space previously made: e.g., ch-1 space	rnd(s)	round(s)
		RS	right side
ch-sp	chain space	sc	single crochet
cm	centimeter(s)	sc2tog	single crochet 2 stitches together
cont	continue	sk	skip
dc	double crochet	Sl st	slip sitich
dc2tog	double crochet 2 stitches together	sp(s)	space(s)
dec	decrease	st(s)	stitch(es)
FL	front loop(s)	tog	together
hdc	half double crochet	WS	wrong side
		yo	yarn over

Crochet Chart Symbols

Crochet patterns may contain stitch charts. These charts are used along with, or instead of, written instructions. These are internationally recognized symbols. Patterns may include additional stitches as well. Read your patterns carefully before you begin!

The symbols represent stitches as they look on the right side of your project.

Standard Stitch Key

$\bigcirc$ = chain (ch)

• = slip stitch (sl st)

X or + = single crochet (sc)*

T = half double crochet (hdc)

T = double crochet (dc)

T = treble crochet (tr)

T = double treble crochet (dtr)

⋏⋏ = sc2tog

⋏⋏⋏ = sc3tog

⋏⋏ = dc3tog

⋏ = dc2tog

T = front post dc (FPdc)

T = back post dc (BPdc)

⌒ = worked in back loop only**

⌣ = worked in front loop only**

*both symbols are commonly used for single crochet
**symbol appears at base of stitch being worked

Read More

Heidenreich, Franziska. *Crochet for Kids: Basic Techniques and Great Projects that Kids Can Make Themselves.* Mechanicsburg, Penn.: Stackpole Books, 2014.

Kustowski, Alex. *Cool Crocheting for Kids: A Fun and Creative Introduction to Fiber Art.* Minneapolis: ABDO Publishing Company, 2015.

Author Bio

Karen Whooley is an award winning, internationally known crochet designer, author, and instructor. She develops patterns and teaches classes for crocheters who want simplicity and elegance wrapped up in adventure.

Karen is the author of *A Garden of Shawls, Crochet Rocks Socks,* and 18 other books as well as many patterns published in books and magazines. Her classes both online and live are some of the most sought after in the crochet genre. Crochet is her passion and she wants to take that passion and inspire crocheters in any way she can. Most importantly, Karen wants to bring each crocheter self-confidence and enable them to take what they have learned from her designs and classes so that they can happily create whatever spurs their own crochet passion.

Find Karen at http://www.KarenWhooley.com

Titles in this Set